COCAINE

Sarah Lennard-Brown

WITHDRAWN

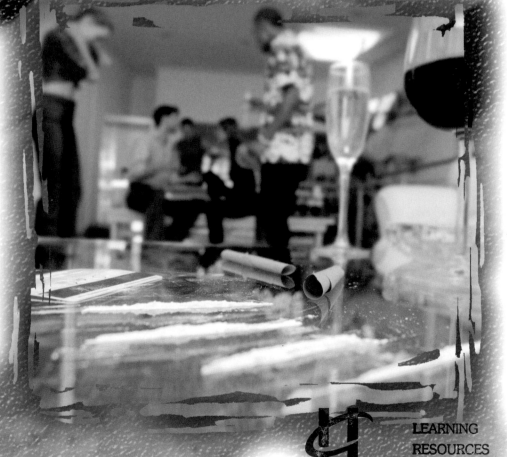

LEARNING
RESOURCES
CENTRE

HAVERING
COLLEGE

HODDER
Wayland

an imprint of Hodder Children's Books

White-Thomson Publishing Ltd,
2-3 St Andrew's Place, Lewes,
East Sussex BN7 1UP

Published in Great Britain in 2004 by Hodder
Wayland, an imprint of Hodder Children's
Books

This book was produced for White-Thomson
Publishing Ltd by Ruth Nason.

Design: Carole Binding
Picture research: Glass Onion Pictures

British Library Cataloguing in Publication Data
Lennard-Brown, Sarah
    Cocaine. - (Health Issues)
    1. Cocaine - Juvenile literature
    2. Cocaine habit - Juvenile literature
    I. Title
    362.2'98

ISBN 0 7502 4485 2

Printed in China by C&C Offset Printing Co., Ltd.

Hodder Children's Books
A division of Hodder Headline Limited
338 Euston Road, London NW1 3BH

Acknowledgements

The author and publishers thank the following for their permission to reproduce photographs and
illustrations: Camera Press: page 16; Corbis: cover and pages 1, 4 (Charles Gupton), 14 (Historical
Picture Archive), 28 (Nancy Ney), 33 (Annie Griffiths Belt), 36 (Ant Strack), 37 (Tom Stewart), 39
(Bill Gentile), 50 (Steve Starr), 52 (Tom Nebbia), 57 (Tom and Dee Ann McCarthy); Angela Hampton
Family Life Picture Library: page 59; Impact: pages 7 (Vera Lentz), 49 (Simon Shepheard); Mediscan:
page 24; Popperfoto: page 12; Rex Features: pages 18 (Patrick Barth), 20 (Sipa Press), 22 (Chat), 31
(Raguet/Phanie), 55 (Sipa Press); Science Photo Library: pages 5 (Wesley Bocxe), 43 (Pascal
Goetgheluck), 45 (Oscar Burriel); Topham/Fotomas: page 10; Topham/ImageWorks: pages 3, 19, 41,
46 (MR©John Griffin). The illustrations on pages 27 and 32 are by Carole Binding.

Note: Photographs illustrating the case studies in this book were posed by models.

Every effort has been made to trace copyright holders. However, the publishers apologise for any
unintentional omissions and would be pleased in such cases to add an acknowledgement in any
future editions.

Contents

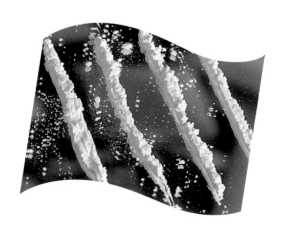

Introduction
What is cocaine?

So much myth and fantasy have been woven around cocaine and its more recent derivatives, crack and freebase, that it can be difficult to separate fact from fiction. Cocaine was traditionally associated with the rich and famous. It was supposed to be the drug of choice for pop stars and celebrities. It was so expensive that using it was a sign of how wealthy you were. There are plenty of stories of parties with bowls of cocaine handed around and cocaine-fuelled poolside revels.

The truth is not so glamorous. Cocaine, crack and freebase are used by street gangs and the poorest members of society, as well as by the rich. They are all extremely addictive. Crack cocaine is reputedly the most addictive drug there is. People who become addicted to these drugs enter a world where the only thing that matters is the next dose of drug and they would do anything to get the money to buy more. Life is dangerous and often violent when they are 'high', and fearful, sad, lonely and miserable when they are not.

The high life
A popular image of cocaine has been that it is used mainly by the wealthy, including highly paid business-people.

Cocaine, crack, freebase and drug mixes

Cocaine *is usually produced as a crystalline white powder, though occasionally it is sold in the form of a paste. It is usually taken by sniffing the powder into the nose, known as 'snorting'.*

Crack cocaine *consists of large crystals, varying from white to a pinky yellow.*

Freebase *is sold as a white powder, and does not have as many impurities in it as crack or cocaine. Crack and freebase are usually smoked, or heated and inhaled.*

Drug mixes *include one known as speedballs (a mixture of cocaine and heroin).*

Cocaine, crack and freebase are Class A Schedule 2 drugs in UK law and Schedule 1 Narcotics in the USA. This means that they are illegal drugs and you can be prosecuted if you are found in possession of them.

The story of cocaine

Cocaine is made from a substance extracted from the leaves of coca plants, which grow in South America. From early times, people living in the Andes mountains have chewed the leaves for the stimulating effects this gives. However, it was not until the 1850s that scientists purified the stimulant substance and created the drug called cocaine. There were high hopes of the new drug, particularly in the development of anaesthetics. At the same time, people began to use the drug for its mind-changing effects. In Chapter 1, you can find out more about the story of cocaine and the way attitudes towards its use have changed over time.

Market increase
Crack and freebase were developed by dealers keen to find more people ready to afford their drugs.

Affecting the mind and body

Drugs that affect the brain, and therefore the mood and behaviour of the user, are called psychoactive. Cocaine, crack and freebase are psychoactive drugs that have a stimulant effect: this means that they make the user feel exhilarated, euphoric and confident. People often become very talkative when they have taken cocaine, and may feel very strong and energetic. However, they may feel anxious and panicky. Cocaine can cause people to become violent and to have severe mental problems. Cocaine can also kill. Chapter 2 studies how cocaine, crack and freebase affect the brain and the rest of the body and the experience of pleasure.

Addiction

Cocaine and its related drugs activate the parts of the brain that are activated by normal pleasures, and this is why the drugs are highly addictive. Users experience pleasure when they take the drug, followed by absence of pleasure. This absence of pleasure is actually the result of having taken cocaine, but the user does not realize this and takes more cocaine to feel better again. The person may become dependent on cocaine to feel any pleasure at all. In Chapters 3 and 4, you can find out more about addiction to cocaine, and how it can be treated.

Cocaine in today's world

In the final chapter we investigate the impact of cocaine, crack and freebase on our world today. A very small proportion of the world's total population ever try cocaine, and yet the drug has a profound impact on the lives and health of many people. For example, there are the people who live with addicts or in areas where crack users congregate. There are also those who live in cocaine-producing areas or who get caught up in drug-smuggling operations. On pages 58-59, we think about the real decisions that affect our lives today and evaluate the risks people take when they decide to try cocaine.

Street names

Cocaine
Coke, nose, blow, snow, snowflake, white lady, lady, Charlie, Candy, Big C, Lines, Peruvian marching powder, Bolivian marching powder.

Crack
Rocks, pebbles, scuds, flake, cloud nine, gravel, nuggets, Roxanne, bomb, coco puffs, dime pieces.

Freebase
Base, baseball, freebase, beat, biscuit, bones, flame throwers.

1 The story of cocaine use
Past into present

Cocaine is produced from the leaves of the South American coca bush *Erythroxylum coca*. The bush grows wild at high altitudes where there is substantial rainfall, such as in the Andes mountains of Colombia, Bolivia and Peru. It is grown legally and illegally in these countries, in blocks of two to three acres called 'cocals'. It is also grown illegally in mountainous areas of South East Asia and India.

Chewing coca leaves

Coca bush leaves have been chewed by the people of South America for about 5,000 years. They discovered that the stimulating effect of chewing the leaves could help them survive the cold, hunger and unpleasant physical sensations they experienced when climbing high into the mountains. Coca leaves contain a very low level of the active substance that makes cocaine so powerful. Each leaf contains approximately 2 per cent of the substance, locked within the cell structure of the plant. To release the

Harvesting
In Peru, it is legal to harvest coca leaves, for chewing and to make coca tea.

substance, the Andes people developed a special method of chewing the coca leaf. First they made lime, by burning seashells. They ground it to a fine powder and kept it in a hollowed-out gourd hung around their waist. The gourd was sealed with a stick that dipped down into the lime. The coca user would lick the stick, dip it into the lime and spread a small layer of lime onto a leaf. The leaf was then folded and chewed slowly for about 45 minutes. Afterwards, the waste was spat out.

Coca leaves were chewed in the same sort of way as people today drink coffee or tea. Coca was chewed after a meal and between meals. The use of coca leaves was so much a part of life in the Andes that, for many tribes, getting your own gourd and coca pouch was a sign of manhood.

In the sixteenth century Spanish invaders reached South America and much of the continent became part of the

Cocaine Timeline

c. 3000 BC	Coca chewing becomes popular among the people of the Andes.
AD 1400s	The Inca people of Peru farm coca.
Early 1500s	Inca coca plantations are taken over by Spanish invaders. The Spanish authorities tax coca production. Reports of the properties of the coca leaf reach Europe.
c. 1575	Labourers in South American silver mines are given coca leaves as payment.
1708	Coca is included in a dictionary of medicinal plants by German Herman Boerhaave.
1855	Cocaine is extracted from coca leaves by German scientist Friedrich Gaedcke.
1859	The extraction process is improved by Albert Niemann.
1862	Merck produces a quarter-pound of refined cocaine.
1869	Seeds of the coca plant become part of the botanical collection at Kew Gardens, London.
1880	Russian doctor Vasili von Anrep discovers the anaesthetizing properties of cocaine.

Spanish empire. At first, the Spanish tried to outlaw the use of coca. Christian priests felt that it was sinful and that it encouraged immoral behaviour and laziness. Eventually, though, Spanish officials saw an opportunity for making money and took over the production of coca leaf. It was used as a form of currency, for example to pay workers in the silver and gold mines. It is still common practice and lawful for people in the Andes to chew coca leaf, but cocaine production and use are illegal, as they are in the rest of the world.

Chewing coca leaves did not catch on in Europe. The leaves did not travel well. They became stale and unusable after the long sea journey to Spain. Also, chewing and spitting were (and still are) considered bad manners in most European countries and the USA.

Legal use

The Peruvian government authorizes farmers to cultivate small amounts of coca leaves, for the purposes of chewing the leaves and for making coca-leaf tea.

1884	Cocaine is first used as a local anaesthetic in eye surgery. The psychiatrist Sigmund Freud publishes his ideas about cocaine in a book called **On Coca.**
1886	Coca-Cola® drink is launched onto the market, containing cocaine syrup and caffeine.
1901	Cocaine is removed from Coca-Cola® recipe.
1905	It becomes fashionable to snort cocaine.
1909	Cocaine is used on the Antarctic expedition of Sir Ernest Shackleton.
1910	Medical journals first report cases of nasal damage due to snorting cocaine.
1911	US government reports 5,000 cocaine-related deaths.
1924	Second International Opium Conference at The Hague includes cocaine in a list of drugs whose production and use should be reduced.
1976	Freebase cocaine is developed.
1980s	Crack cocaine is developed. It and freebase become popular.
2000	Crack and freebase begin to replace ecstasy in Britain and Europe as a nightclub dance drug.

The creation of cocaine

Cocaine itself was not produced until 1855, when the German scientist Friedrich Gaedcke worked out how to extract and purify the active substance from the coca leaf. Another German, Albert Niemann, improved the process in 1859. Both scientists were interested in the medical properties of the drug, particularly its ability to relieve pain. At this time there were no real anaesthetics to prevent patients from feeling pain during surgery. Surgery had to be carried out very fast or the patient would die as a result of the pain. The need to work so fast made it impossible for surgeons to be very careful and accurate. Therefore, the search for an anaesthetic that would allow less painful, more accurate surgery was very important. In 1880, a Russian doctor, Vasili von Anrep, discovered the anaesthetizing properties of cocaine and the Western world became increasingly interested in the drug.

Sigmund Freud recommends cocaine

One of the most famous people to become fascinated with the new drug was the psychiatrist Sigmund Freud. In 1884 he published *On Coca*, the first study of the effects of cocaine. While living in Vienna (Austria), he

Dental agony
Before the introduction of anaesthetics, doctors and dentists could do little to lessen the pain of surgery. Alcohol was generally used to dull the patient's senses.

experimented with taking the drug himself and recorded what happened. At first he was very enthusiastic. The drug gave him lots of energy and made him feel euphoric, and he felt that it might help his friend, Ernst von Fleischl-Marxow, to overcome his addiction to the drug morphine. This was a disaster. Ernst quickly became heavily addicted to cocaine. He took more and more, becoming the first person on record to develop a mental illness called cocaine-induced psychosis. In this illness the sufferer experiences disturbing and frightening thoughts which seem so real to them that they may behave in strange and frightening ways. After this, Freud's opinion of cocaine changed and he regarded it as potentially dangerous.

Freud helped the development of ophthalmic (eye) surgery when he reported the anaesthetic qualities of cocaine to his friend, ophthalmologist (eye specialist) Carl Koller. Cocaine paste (a more dilute form of cocaine) was found to be very useful as a local anaesthetic in eye surgery. It is still used as a local anaesthetic in some eye, ear, nose and dental operations today. It is sometimes mixed with other drugs and applied directly to the area requiring anaesthetic.

Sigmund Freud – revolutionary ideas

Sigmund Freud (1856-1939) studied medicine at the University of Vienna and eventually specialized in psychiatry. Some case studies about hysteria that he wrote in the 1890s are thought to be the first examples of psychoanalysis. This is where a psychiatrist helps the patient to find the cause of their problems through discussion. Freud felt that many psychiatric problems were caused by childhood trauma and unconscious urges and needs. These ideas were revolutionary for the time. Between 1896 and 1901, Freud worked on the detail of his theory of psychoanalysis and developed more new ideas about how our minds work. It was Freud who came up with the notion of the unconscious and conscious mind and who first examined how our experiences affect the way we think and act.

Popular use of cocaine

Around 1880, many new products containing small amounts of processed cocaine became available across America and Europe. These included syrups and wines, tonics and lozenges for treating coughs and sore throats. In 1886 a new drink, Coca-Cola®, was released onto the

market, made from a secret recipe including cocaine-laced syrup and caffeine. It rapidly became a very popular soft drink and continued to contain cocaine syrup until it was removed from the formula in 1901.

Cocaine became famous for its stimulating properties. Cocaine tablets called 'Forced March' were used by members of the Antarctic expedition led by Sir Ernest Shackleton in 1909. The tablets were to help the explorers keep going under difficult conditions. Cocaine products were also used to improve the endurance of athletes, especially runners. In the early twentieth century cocaine was used by athletes in preparation for matches as well as training. This was before people became aware of the dangers of cocaine, or of issues about drug use in sport.

Changing ideas about drug use

In the late nineteenth century, experimenting with drugs was not considered shocking and was not illegal. However, taking drugs was disapproved of and thought to be a sign of 'moral depravity' or a 'weak mind'. In 1887 the British writer Sir Arthur Conan Doyle published the first of many

Antarctic survival

Sir Ernest Shackleton (1874-1922) made four expeditions to the Antarctic. In 1909, when he almost reached the South Pole, he and his team of explorers took tablets containing cocaine, to help them endure the polar conditions.

stories about the fictional detective Sherlock Holmes. In the stories, Holmes is addicted to cocaine and the narrator, Dr Watson, warns him of the (then) little-known dangers of long-term cocaine use. Holmes eventually manages to stop using cocaine in the stories in 1896. Conan Doyle is sometimes criticized for portraying a hero as a drug user. However, others feel that he was showing the spirit of self-experimentation that was common at the time.

Snorting (sniffing cocaine into the nose) became popular around 1905, when patents taken out by the company E. Merck, on the process of producing cocaine, expired. This meant that anyone could now make cocaine, using Merck's process. Cocaine became cheaper and started to be used by the young and wealthy in Europe and America. In 1910, British medical journals included the first reports of nasal damage due to snorting and, in 1912, the US government recorded more than 5,000 deaths due to cocaine use in one year.

During the late nineteenth and early twentieth centuries, the world was waking up to the health and social problems caused by drug addiction. Addiction to opium had already caused enormous problems in China and Egypt. Now the availability of narcotic drugs was seen to be causing a growing rate of addiction and many deaths in Europe and the USA. Representatives of many countries discussed how to tackle the international drugs problem. At the Second International Opium Conference in 1924, they agreed to make laws to try to reduce the use of narcotic drugs. Over the following decades, many countries outlawed the production, sale and possession of drugs including heroin, cocaine, opium and cannabis. However, there were still people prepared to break the law and risk prison because they saw a chance to make a large profit, selling the drugs to people who were addicted or could be persuaded to try them. It is illegal to grow coca leaves in nearly all countries, except some in South America, such as Peru and Bolivia, where small-scale growing of coca is allowed on cultural and religious grounds.

Cocaine in popular culture

References to cocaine in popular music and culture are evidence that it has been a fashionable drug. First the drug was featured in the Sherlock Holmes stories by Sir Arthur Conan Doyle, in the late nineteenth century. In the 1930s a song by Cole Porter, 'I get a kick out of you', referred to cocaine directly as a substance used by some people to get a 'kick'. The drug came into fashion again after the Second World War, with the psychedelic movement, and in the 1970s, at which time Eric Clapton released the song 'Cocaine'.

Elementary

For the first ten years of writing his Sherlock Holmes stories, Sir Arthur Conan Doyle presented the fictional detective as a cocaine user.

In and out of fashion

Because it is expensive to import and refine, cocaine is an expensive drug. Only rich people could afford to buy it, and so taking cocaine became a sign that someone was wealthy. In the 1920s, after the First World War, society in Europe and the USA was sharply divided between rich and poor. As the poor struggled to make a living, the rich (or, more often, the children of the rich) tried to forget the horror and grief of the war and had the time, money and contacts to buy cocaine. However, the dangers of cocaine soon became obvious. Because it was rich and famous people who died from cocaine overdose, their stories appeared in the newspapers. People therefore became aware of the problems associated with cocaine, and it fell out of fashion. By the 1940s a police officer working as a narcotics supervisor in New York reported that he rarely heard of cocaine being used.

In the 1950s the situation changed again. The world was recovering from the Second World War. Young people had more money to spend than ever before and were determined to forget the experience of wartime. Once more, cocaine use shot up and then rapidly decreased once the dangers and addictions became obvious.

The development of crack and freebase

In the 1970s and 1980s new forms of cocaine, called crack and freebase, were developed by dealers looking for more people to sell their drugs to. Crack and freebase were easily made from cocaine, and the method produced a greater amount of drug – although this was largely made up of baking soda, which was used in the process. The new forms of cocaine could be smoked. The effects were felt more quickly, but lasted for a shorter time, than when cocaine was snorted. Cocaine and crack became popular among drug addicts in Hollywood and fashionable again. Because crack and freebase were cheaper to produce, they were seen as 'downmarket'. They became popular among gangs in inner-city areas of the USA. Cocaine became briefly popular among wealthy city business people in the USA and Europe and celebrities who could afford it. Then the addiction and dangers were publicized in the media and the drug went out of fashion again.

'Smoking crack – it's hard to describe. You go from heaven to hell in the space of fifteen minutes. It changes your head, it's a road to disaster. Don't do it.' (Sonny, aged 21, recovering crack addict)

The price of cocaine

Since cocaine was first produced in 1862, its price has varied enormously. Sometimes it is very expensive, due to the difficulty growing, processing and smuggling it and the high profits demanded by 'drug bosses'. Between 1990 and 2000 the street price of a gram of cocaine varied between approximately £40 and £100. Since 1990 the prices of cocaine, crack and freebase have come down. Crack cocaine is sold in 'rocks' – large crystals which can be subdivided into 'boulders' and 'pebbles'. A rock of crack sold for between £5 and £30 during the 1990s and between $5 and $20 in the USA.

Where does cocaine come from today?

The United Nations estimates that the world's cultivation of coca leaves went down by 17 per cent between 1990 and 1997. Most cocaine production takes place in the South American countries of Peru, Colombia and Bolivia, with some smaller areas of production in Brazil, Guyana and Venezuela. There was a 40 per cent reduction of cocaine production in Peru in the 1990s. Bolivia has reduced the area of land producing coca leaf by 50 per cent. However, coca leaf production in Colombia has increased.

Colombia is now responsible for two-thirds of the world's coca leaf production and about 80 per cent of cocaine manufacture. Gangs of people who produce, smuggle and supply cocaine are known as drug cartels and are usually led by powerful drug bosses or 'drug barons'. The cartels are very rich and pay for mercenaries (hired soldiers) to protect the areas where they grow cocaine. This leads to violence and conflict, and the people in these areas live in fear and uncertainty.

'There is often fighting around my town. People are killed and their homes are burnt. The rebels grow coca in the mountains and are trying to take control of this area away from the government.' (Gabrielle, aged 10, Colombian student)

Daily life in Colombia

Rebel soldiers patrol a town in Colombia. Fighting between rebels (funded by cocaine smuggling) and the government in Colombia has been going on for more than 40 years. Over 30,000 people have been killed in the fighting.

The vast majority of the cocaine produced in South America is smuggled into the USA, while smaller amounts go to Europe and Australia. Of the total amount of cocaine seized by the police in 1997-98, 83 per cent was seized in the USA and 11 per cent in Europe.

Who uses cocaine?

A lot fewer people use cocaine than you might expect from its high profile in the media. The United Nations Office on Drugs and Crime estimates that 180 million people worldwide over the age of 15 consumed drugs at some point during the late 1990s. This is about 4.2 per cent of the world's population. The most commonly used drug was cannabis (144 million users), followed by amphetamine-type stimulants (29 million users). By contrast, cocaine had only 14 million users worldwide (approximately 0.3 per cent of the world's population).

Drug use around the world

Drug	% of world population using the drug during 1990s (over 15)
All illegal drugs	4.2%
Cannabis	3.3%
Amphetamines	0.7%
Cocaine	0.3%

(The United Nations Office on Drugs and Crime World Drug Report 2000)

During the late twentieth century cocaine use around the world was stable or decreasing, except in a few areas. It is thought that cocaine consumption fell by 70 per cent in the USA between 1985 and 1999. The only places where cocaine use increased were certain areas in 'transit countries' such as Mexico, other central and southern American countries, parts of southern and western Africa and Eastern Europe. Transit countries are the countries used by the drug cartels to smuggle cocaine into the USA, Western Europe and Australia. Since the end of the twentieth century, cocaine use in the UK seems to have risen: customs officers seized more cocaine than heroin, and 6 per cent of people between the ages of 16 and 29 tried the drug, compared with 1 per cent who tried heroin or crack cocaine (according to the British Crime Survey, 1999).

Working out who takes cocaine in the general population is difficult. Most cocaine users are occasional users and do not come to the attention of the authorities or health services. Therefore they do not appear in official drug use statistics. Cocaine remains fairly expensive and so its users tend to be wealthy. If they need treatment for their cocaine habit, they tend to pay for it privately and, again, they are not recorded in the statistics. There is no quick medical cure for cocaine addiction, and so there is little incentive for addicts to approach drug agencies for help. Regular surveys by the UK charity DrugScope have found that there is little use of cocaine among schoolchildren or older adults, but that up to a quarter of people attending nightclubs have tried cocaine.

It seems that the majority of cocaine users across the world are white males between the ages of 16 and 24, living in urban areas. The number of women reporting ever having tried cocaine is approximately half the number of men. Use of cocaine by groups younger than 16 and older than 35 is negligible.

Dance scene cocaine use

'It always used to be ecstasy that people offered you at clubs. Some of my friends used to do it, but I never fancied it. I didn't like the risk – we'd all heard about people who died after taking one ecstasy tablet, and so I never took any. But now it's changing. I suppose because no one took ecstasy any more, they tried something new. I didn't realize coke was dangerous. The bloke who sold it said it couldn't harm you. I'd just feel fantastic. Well I did feel fantastic at first, and it stopped me eating. But later I'd feel terrible – there was nothing worse. A friend of mine told me about what she'd learnt at school, about it being addictive like heroin and stuff. So I stopped. It's no good taking things that mess with your head. And you can never believe those dealers – they'd say anything if it made you buy some.'
(Leanne, clubber)

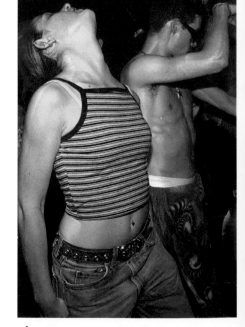

2 The effects of cocaine
Risks to body and mind

How do people take cocaine?

Cocaine is usually sold in the form of a white powder. The user takes it by snorting, which means sniffing the powder into the nose. It is absorbed by the mucous membranes lining the nose, and from here it enters the bloodstream and travels to the brain. Another method some people use to take the cocaine powder is to rub it onto their gums or other mucous membranes.

Some people inject cocaine into their body. This involves dissolving the drug in a liquid and injecting it either into a vein or into the fat layer just below the skin. When the drug is injected into a vein, it gets into the bloodstream immediately and so its effects are felt much faster than with other methods. As with injecting any drug, there are risks of infection with viruses such as hepatitis and HIV, if needles are not sterile. Injecting can also damage veins and arteries. To make cocaine dissolve in a fluid, so that it can be injected, the mixture has to be heated. However, cocaine is easily broken down by heat. For this reason, injecting cocaine is not a popular method of taking the drug, as it is easy to destroy the cocaine and waste a lot of money in the process.

Preparing cocaine

Taking cocaine is often made into a ritual, using the same procedure every time. Some users always use the same equipment, such as a particular mirror or china plate. Some always use a credit card, or a razor blade, to arrange the lines of drug for snorting. Some people snort cocaine from a specially shaped spoon.

Dangers of injecting cocaine

Apart from the danger of overdosing, the biggest risk in injecting cocaine comes from sharing needles and syringes with other drug users. Body fluids on shared equipment can pass infections such as HIV and hepatitis B and C from one person to another. Other dangers include infections at the injection site, septicaemia (a life-threatening infection of the blood), endocarditis (an infection of the heart) and gangrene (a bacterial infection). Injecting can also damage tissue around the injection site, especially if the same areas are used repeatedly, and eventually the tissue may die (necrosis). Repeated tissue damage from injections can also lead to blood clots in the veins (thrombosis) and inflammation of veins (phlebitis).

In many countries there are needle exchange schemes which aim to reduce the spread of diseases like HIV and hepatitis. They allow injecting drug users to exchange their dirty needles for sterile ones and encourage them to use the new needle only once.

Coca paste is rare, but it is usually smoked in a pipe called a bhong. Again, because cocaine breaks down when it is heated, the effects of the drug are reduced by this method.

How do people take crack and freebase?

Crack and freebase are able to withstand the temperatures reached during smoking. However, if the smoking temperature becomes too high, even these forms of cocaine will break down and the drug will not produce the desired effect. Therefore, crack and freebase smokers have developed several methods to try to keep the temperature as low as possible. Some use bhongs, which are also commonly used by cannabis smokers. These pipes have a water-filled chamber through which the vapour is drawn before it is inhaled. Another method of taking crack and freebase is to place the drug in a glass

Vapours

Crack or freebase are sometimes warmed in a glass tube or pipe and the vapours inhaled.

tube or on glass or metal foil and warm it with a match or lighter. This produces a vapour, which the user then inhales.

Immediate effects

Cocaine is a stimulant drug, and that is exactly what it does to the body. It stimulates it, speeding everything up. People who have taken cocaine become very active and talkative. They feel energetic and have a sense of euphoria (an extreme sense of wellbeing), which can be very pleasurable. Users often claim that they can see things remarkably clearly when they have taken the drug. This

Effects of taking cocaine

Short-term effects	Long-term effects	Overdose
Energy	Heart disease	Irregular heartbeat
Euphoria	Stroke	Convulsions
Talkative	Damage to the nasal septum,	Coma
Heightened awareness	the strip of tissue that	Heart failure
of surroundings	divides the nose into	Respiratory arrest
Feelings of strength	nostrils	(stops breathing)
Fast heartbeat	Depression	Death
High blood pressure	Anxiety	
Facial numbness	Cocaine psychosis (strange	
Tremors (shaking)	and frightening thoughts	
Headache	that can result in strange	
Faster breathing	and violent behaviour)	
Anxiety	Paranoia	
Irritability	Hallucinations	
Paranoia	Stereotypical movements	
Depression	(repetitive picking or	
Weakness	stroking of body parts)	
Increased chance of stroke	Infertility	
and heart attack	Malnutrition	
	Infections	

feeling, which is just another effect of the drug, can mislead people into making unsafe decisions, for example to participate in casual sex or dangerous stunts. Cocaine stimulates all the systems of the body, including the heart rate and blood pressure, and this can be very dangerous.

Although the effects of cocaine are felt almost immediately, they can take 30 minutes to develop fully after snorting. The drug is broken down by the body very fast so, within an hour, about half of the dose has broken down and is no longer capable of affecting the brain. Cocaine mimics the effects of the body's sympathetic nervous system. This is sometimes called the 'fight or flight' mechanism, because it primes your body to stand and fight or run away from danger. It speeds up your heart and makes sure your muscles have lots of energy (glucose) so that you can run fast. It also makes your lungs breathe more quickly and efficiently, to supply extra oxygen to the muscles so that they can operate effectively. Cocaine

Crash landing
When the first effects of cocaine wear off, the user is left feeling weak, anxious and depressed.

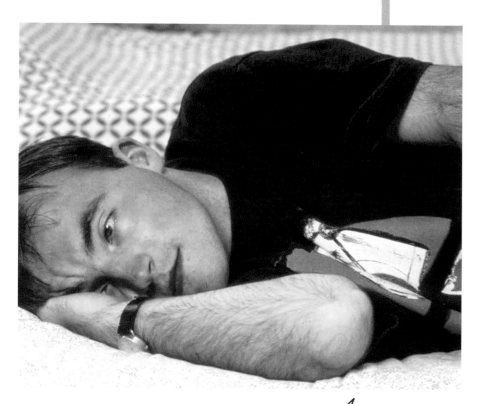

causes massive activation of the 'fight or flight' system, to the extent that it can cause an irregular heartbeat, a heart attack or a stroke (where a blood clot causes the death of some brain tissue). All of these can be fatal.

The massive high produced by cocaine is followed by an equally massive low, as the drug passes through the user's system. Users are left feeling weak, anxious and depressed. This 'crash' often makes them want to take more of the drug, in order to feel good again, and so a cycle of using starts. The high-low cycle can lead a user to keep on taking the drug until they have none left or until their system becomes so poisoned by the drug that they die.

The dangers of snorting

When cocaine is snorted, the user may notice that, at first, their face becomes numb, a feeling that passes after a few minutes. This is because of the anaesthetizing properties of cocaine. Over time, snorting cocaine damages the

'You can never tell exactly what a "hit" will be like. It depends how strong the cocaine is and what it's been cut with. Sometimes I don't think there's any coke in it at all. Other times it's so strong, it's scary.' (Eva, aged 18, regular cocaine user)

The risks of adulterated drugs

Cocaine powder is rarely 100 per cent pure – in other words, not all the powder is actually cocaine. Dealers have usually diluted it, to varying degrees, with a 'filler' substance, something that is a white powder like cocaine but not as expensive. This puts the user at risk in several ways. Firstly, they can never be sure how strong the drug is. If they take cocaine that has not been diluted as much as they are used to, it is possible that they will overdose.

Another risk is from the substances used as filler. Sometimes this is white flour or talcum powder or other cheaper drugs such as amphetamines. None of these substances is harmless. Snorting flour or talc into your lungs can cause lung disease. Some substances used as filler can cause severe injury or kill you.

nose. The drug causes the blood vessels in the nose to narrow. Blood supply is therefore reduced and ulcers can develop inside the nose. As the ulcers spread, long-term cocaine snorting leads to the gradual destruction of the nasal septum, the strip of cartilage that separates the nostrils. Some heavy cocaine users are left with a very large hole in the nasal septum, which may need surgical repair.

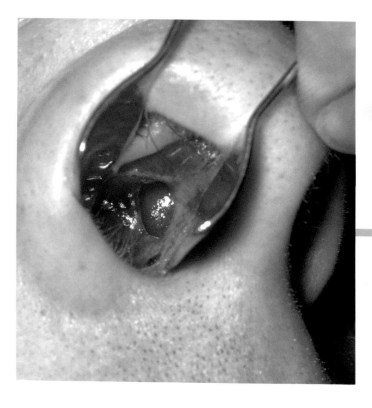

Blood vessels

The narrowing of blood vessels is called vasoconstriction. Taking cocaine causes vasoconstriction in the nose, in the lining of the stomach and even in the intestines, leading to ulcers and internal bleeding.

Nasal damage
A damaged nasal septum affects the person's breathing. It also alters the way they sound when speaking or singing. This has happened to some rock stars who have been heavy cocaine users.

Cocaine and heart disease
Heart disease can result from long-term cocaine use, as the drug speeds up the development of fatty deposits (atherosclerosis) inside blood vessels. As the fatty deposits increase, the heart has to work harder to pump the blood through narrower tubes. This can cause the heart to grow larger (the heart muscle gets bigger as it has to work harder) and weaker, resulting in heart failure. Also, as the fatty deposits become larger, they can either block a blood vessel entirely or they can break off and travel through the

blood system until they get lodged in a narrow blood vessel. This can cause a stroke (a blockage in the blood vessels of the brain) or a heart attack. Deep vein thrombosis (a blockage of the veins in the leg) or pulmonary embolism (a blockage of the blood supply to the lungs) can be caused by complications following injecting cocaine into a vein. All of these can be fatal or can leave the person with permanent disability.

The effect of cocaine on mental health

Cocaine can affect the mental health of users. Long-term cocaine users tend to have an increased level of paranoia (feeling that people are out to get them) and can suffer from severe depression. Some long-term users experience a condition called cocaine psychosis, where they lose contact with reality, are haunted by fear and have hallucinations. These hallucinations often involve the idea that there are insects trapped under their skin. In order to get rid of these unreal creatures, the person may scratch at their skin, giving themselves large wounds. People with cocaine psychosis are often aggressive and violent and may require hospital treatment to prevent them harming themselves or others.

Like a wild animal

'The night Andy flipped out was one of the scariest of my life. We'd been out clubbing and having a good time. I knew Andy did coke occasionally, but I don't like drugs so he didn't tell me he'd scored (bought some) and snorted it in the washroom. He was OK for a while, a bit hyper, dancing like crazy – but Andy's like that. Then everything went mad. He started saying that the barman was after him, that his drinks were poisoned and that we had to protect him. He was really scared and jumpy. We tried to get him home, but then he turned on us, saying we were going to kill him. One of my mates held his arm and he hit out like a wild animal. We couldn't hold him and he ran off. The police picked him up eventually. It was terrible – I didn't know drugs could do that to you.'
(Steve, aged 24, mechanic)

Some other long-term effects of cocaine use

There are some problems associated with using cocaine, which are not directly caused by the drug. Cocaine tends to reduce appetite and increase activity, and so long-term users are often tired and undernourished. As a result, their resistance to infectious diseases is reduced. They tend to become ill more often and take longer to recover.

Patterns of behaviour caused by using cocaine have a health cost, too. Cocaine use can increase the desire for sexual intercourse. This may result in the user having unprotected sex with many different partners. Some people may become involved in prostitution in order to get money to pay for cocaine. This puts people at high risk of developing sexually transmitted diseases including HIV.

The action of cocaine in the brain

Cocaine use has a profound effect on the way the brain works. The effects of cocaine, including feeling good (euphoria), fast heart beat, decreased appetite and increased ability to concentrate, all occur because the drug stimulates the production of a group of chemicals in the brain called monoamine neurotransmitters. These chemicals are involved in transmitting signals between different nerves in the brain. Nerves are the structures in your body that communicate between your body and brain, and this is one of the ways in which your brain can control what your body is doing. For example, if you want to pick up a pencil, your brain sends messages through your network of nerves to tell the muscles of your arm and fingers what to do. There are many nerves around your body and they all pass information to your brain. Neurotransmitters are the chemicals in your brain that pass the message on from one nerve in the brain to the next.

The neurotransmitters affected by cocaine include serotonin, noradrenalin and dopamine. Cocaine increases the amount of these neurotransmitters at the nerve junctions, called synapses, and this excites the nerve endings so that they send out more signals. The result is

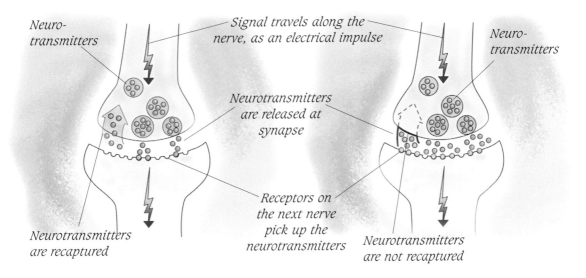

Normal function of nerves in the brain

Neuro-transmitters

Signal travels along the nerve, as an electrical impulse

Neurotransmitters are released at synapse

Neurotransmitters are recaptured

Receptors on the next nerve pick up the neurotransmitters

How cocaine affects this functioning

Neuro-transmitters

Neurotransmitters are not recaptured

that the person feels excitable, jumpy and full of energy. Each neurotransmitter affects different behaviours.

◉ The effects of serotonin

Serotonin helps your body get ready for sleep and plays a big part in regulating your body clock. Your body clock is an important mechanism that keeps your body functioning in rhythm. It controls your body temperature, lowering it at night and raising it in the morning to ensure you have the energy to get out of bed and face the day. It also controls your sleep cycles, helping to make you feel tired in the evening and have the right amount of deep sleep and dream sleep so that you feel refreshed in the morning. Your body clock is also involved in appetite regulation. It makes you feel hungry at certain times when your body is used to being fed, such as at breakfast, lunch and dinner.

Cocaine disrupts the production of serotonin and this upsets the body clock, first making the user feel wide awake at night and taking away their appetite and afterwards leaving them extremely sleepy and hungry.

Cocaine and the neurotransmitters

This is a simplified drawing of how signals are passed from one nerve in the brain to the next, normally (left) and when the person has taken cocaine (right). Cocaine greatly increases the amount of neuro-transmitters that are released at the synapses (junctions between nerves). It also stops the normal process whereby neuro-transmitters are recaptured.

✺ The effects of noradrenalin (norepinephrine)

Noradrenalin is one of several hormones produced when you have a shock. It is related to the hormone adrenaline, which makes your heart beat faster and your skin turn pale and clammy. (Adrenaline production is also triggered by cocaine but this takes place in your adrenal glands, not your brain.) Noradrenalin is involved in controlling the way you behave in an emergency. It regulates the amount of energy available to your muscles and brain. It widens the passages in your lungs to help you get more oxygen into your body. It also helps you to feel full of energy and enthusiasm, and to pay more attention to the world around you, to help you get yourself out of danger. Noradrenalin reduces your appetite because, if you are in danger, it is not helpful to be distracted by hunger.

Cocaine increases the amount of noradrenalin available in the brain and this again stops the user from feeling hungry, speeds up their heart rate and gives what is often described as a 'rush' of excitement.

Happy feelings
Laughing and happy social interaction produce dopamine, the pleasure-giving brain chemical.

⊛ The effects of dopamine

Dopamine is the chemical messenger produced in your brain when you feel happy. If there is not enough dopamine, you feel sad. Dopamine is very important in what doctors call the brain's 'reward system'. According to this idea, dopamine is produced when you do something pleasurable – for example, eating, laughing, dancing or loving – because these things are necessary in order for human beings to survive. For example, eating is essential to keep us alive, and having successful social relations with other people is also essential for our survival as a group. Our brains are thought to have evolved a method of rewarding us for behaviour that helps us survive: producing dopamine so that we experience pleasure when doing these things and want to do them again.

Dopamine is therefore closely bound up with addiction. Cocaine increases the production of dopamine and so people have a powerful sense of pleasure when they take the drug. This feeling wears off as the drug is broken down by the body, but the urge to experience the rush of pleasure is powerful, and so drug addicts want to take the drug again and again. This process is described in more detail in Chapter 3.

Dopamine is also involved in controlling movement. People with Parkinson's disease produce reduced amounts of dopamine, and this lessens their ability to start and stop movements. It can also cause their hands to shake.

When someone takes cocaine, the amount of serotonin, noradrenalin and dopamine at the synapses (nerve junctions) increases dramatically. The result is that the nerves that control the fight or flight response, the heart rate and blood pressure, alertness, movement, euphoria, appetite and body temperature all fire repeatedly. This can be very dangerous for the heart and circulatory system, as it makes them work very hard.

Cocaine does not only cause the brain to produce more neurotransmitters. It also disrupts the normal way in which neurotransmitters work in the brain (see the diagram on page 27). Usually, signals or messages travel through the nerves as electrical impulses. When a signal reaches a synapse, a neurotransmitter is released to pass the signal across the junction to the next nerve. Special receptors on the second nerve pick up the neurotransmitter. But then the first nerve sucks back, or recaptures, the neurotransmitter so that it can be used again. The recapturing of the neurotransmitter is important, as it switches off the nerve signal after the message has been sent. Cocaine stops this happening and so the nerves keep on sending their messages again and again.

'When I crash after a cocaine hit, it's like I've been thrown out of heaven and I've ended up in hell.' (Elisa, aged 17, student)

Taking cocaine results in less neurotransmitter being recaptured. Therefore, after the first effects of the drug have worn off, there is a period when the nerves are not able to work as well as they do normally. The person feels very sleepy, lethargic, cold, depressed and miserable. This 'low' is caused by cocaine, just as much as the initial 'high'. However, this is not always obvious to the cocaine user. They remember the first feelings of energy and euphoria and often, mistakenly, blame the bad feelings on real life. So they want to take more cocaine to feel good again, not realizing that they will also make themselves feel even worse afterwards. This cycle can lead to individuals taking more and more cocaine.

'If there's coke going, I can snort it till it's gone. Once you start, you never want it to end.' (Vince, aged 20, cocaine addict)

Before scientists realized how profoundly cocaine affected people, they performed several experiments with animals to investigate the effects of the drug. They found that animals that could take as much cocaine as they wished continued to take it until they died. The pleasure caused by the drug was so intense that the animals did not stop taking it, even when its toxic effects on their bodies

became uncomfortable. This is very unusual behaviour. Normally, animals stop taking a drug once it becomes physically unpleasant. The strange behaviour of animals taking cocaine is echoed by the experience of many cocaine users, who will continue to take the drug until they run out of it or they overdose.

Overdose

Cocaine works by over-stimulating the nervous system, and it is thought that this effect explains why some cocaine users have convulsions (violent spasms of the body, also known as fits). Convulsions can happen after someone has taken cocaine that is only slightly more concentrated than the dose needed to cause euphoria. It is very easy to overdose on cocaine, because the drug is poisonous at quite low concentrations. Convulsions combined with raised body temperature, a racing heartbeat and high blood pressure can cause cardiac arrest, respiratory failure and death.

Symptoms of a cocaine overdose

The first signs of a cocaine overdose are a flushed (red) face and hot, dry skin. These show that the person's body temperature is rising above normal. The person may also have cramps in their arms and legs and they will feel panicky and anxious. They may become unconscious or start to have convulsions.

ACTION

- *Do not panic, but call an ambulance immediately.*
- *If the person is conscious, talk to them in a calm and reassuring manner. Loosen clothing and try to keep them cool. Do not allow them anything to eat or drink, except for drinking water.*
- *If the person is having convulsions, make sure that they are safe and there is nothing around that they could bump into. Do not touch them until they have stopped fitting. Do not put anything in their mouth.*
- *If the person is unconscious, roll them into the recovery position. Make sure that their airway is not obstructed and stay with them until the ambulance arrives. Keep a watch on the person's breathing, as you may need to start artificial respiration if they stop breathing.*

Cocaine is even more dangerous when it is mixed with other drugs – especially those that affect heart rate or breathing or those that make people more likely to have convulsions. These include heroin, heart disease medication and high levels of caffeine or theophylline (a treatment for asthma).

Cocaine and pregnancy

The use of cocaine during pregnancy is very dangerous to the unborn child. Cocaine causes constriction of the blood vessels that supply oxygen and nutrients from the mother to the baby. As a result, the baby may not be able to grow

Recovery position

To put someone in the recovery position, lie them on their left side, with their right arm and right leg bent. This means that, if they vomit, there is less risk of them choking on it.

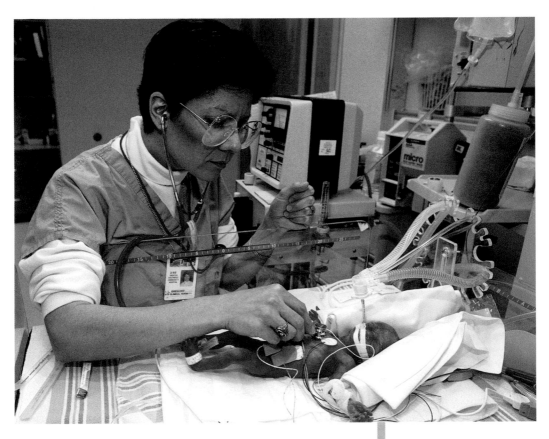

or develop properly in the mother's womb. The pregnancy may then end in miscarriage or stillbirth. Occasionally, babies of mothers who use cocaine are born dependent on the drug. They suffer distressing withdrawal symptoms after they are born. Such babies are usually very small and premature (born too early) and this can put them at increased risk of disease and death in the first weeks of life.

The effects of crack and freebase

Freebase and crack are a stronger form of cocaine, and are much more potent at lower doses. Smoking crack or freebase can cause extreme elation and feelings of power and limitless strength. These effects are felt within seconds and last between 15 minutes and one hour. Some users say that crack and freebase cause the most powerful feelings of any street drug. However, the 'high' is often quickly followed by equally powerful tiredness, weakness

Born to a crack addict
A premature baby born to a crack addict needs intensive care and may not survive.

and feelings of being threatened (sometimes called paranoia). When these profoundly low feelings kick in, the user often wants to take more of the drug immediately, to try to stop the feelings of weakness and anxiety. Of course, if they do take more, they feel good for another 15 minutes or so, but then the bad feeling returns and the high-low cycle continues. Users can often get through many hundreds of pounds worth of drug in one session, despite the low cost of freebase and crack in comparison to cocaine.

'Crack's taken over my life. I spend all day getting money to buy more, or taking it. I don't know how to stop – part of me doesn't want to, but part of me knows that I have to or I'll die.'
(Liam, aged 17, crack addict)

The long-term consequences of using crack and freebase are the same as for cocaine. In addition, smoking the drugs causes narrowing of the blood vessels in the lungs. This can result in ulceration of the lung tissue and cause bleeding.

Heavy use of crack and freebase often leaves users with profound psychological problems. Many develop a deep sense of paranoia, and are suspicious of everyone. They can also be very aggressive, particularly to anyone who tries to stop them taking the drug. They may become violent and have delusions (believe things that are imaginary). For some long-term crack users, these effects can be permanent.

'My brother got in with a gang that did crack. It destroyed him and us. He turned into a monster, lying, stealing. He started hitting us – he attacked Mum with a bread knife when she tried to stop him going out to get drugs. Crack is evil.'
(Shelley, aged 14)

The extreme high produced by crack and freebase makes them very addictive drugs, even more so than cocaine itself. In the next chapter, we investigate the biological mechanisms and other factors that affect addiction. We also investigate withdrawal from cocaine and how people can recover from cocaine addiction.

3 Cocaine addiction
How it develops

Medical experts say that someone is addicted to a drug if they use it repetitively and compulsively, in spite of the negative consequences this has. Substances to which people become addicted activate the basic 'reward system' in the brain, which responds to normal pleasures such as food, sex and love. The system is made up of nerve cells (neurones), and it can be stimulated by an electrical current. Scientific experiments have shown that animals and humans will do an incredible variety of things in order to set off an electric current that stimulates the reward system; in other words, they will do an incredible variety of things in order to have the experience of pleasure. These experiments have helped doctors to understand how addiction works.

The neurotransmitter (brain chemical) dopamine is closely connected with the experience of pleasure. Drugs that are addictive usually directly affect the production of dopamine. As we saw in Chapter 2, cocaine causes large amounts of dopamine to be released into the junctions between nerves. This makes cocaine highly addictive.

The importance of pleasure

Pleasure is very important in our lives. If you think about the activities that give us

Pleasure centres

In 1954, scientists James Olds and Peter Milner discovered that rats could learn how to press a lever in order to set off an electric current that would stimulate the pleasure centres in their brain. Other experiments found that, if rats were forced to choose between food and electrical stimulation of their pleasure centres, they would choose to do without food and starve themselves in order to keep stimulating their pleasure centres.

pleasure naturally, you will see that they usually have some function in helping us survive. We get pleasure from eating a nice meal. When we are very hungry, we get pleasure from eating nearly anything. If we are thirsty, we experience pleasure when we drink.

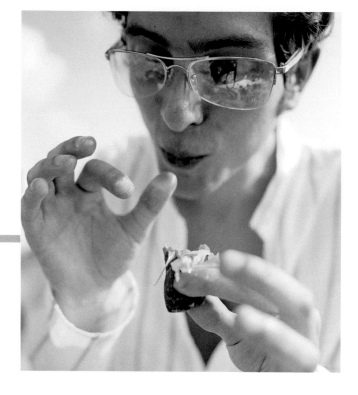

Satisfying hunger
Eating is pleasurable and also necessary for our survival.

What makes a drug addictive?

In order for a drug to be considered addictive, it has to cause one or more of the following things to happen.

- The drug has to affect the user in such a way that they continue to use it regularly and repetitively, despite any unpleasant effects it may have on their bodies or their lives.
- The user has to experience a physical need or a psychological need to use the drug, and the need has to be so strong that they feel compelled to keep on using the drug.
- The drug has to activate the parts of the brain that are activated by normal pleasures, such as food, sex or laughing.
- Usually, the drug has to cause unpleasant symptoms for the user when they stop using it.

Love and sex are sources of pleasure, as are laughing with friends, spending time with loving relatives and exercise. All these things are necessary for our health and social wellbeing. If we did not do these things, our survival as individuals and as a social group would be threatened. Imagine how difficult life would be if there was no love and friendship in the world. Do you think parents would look after their children? Would there be any children? Would anyone work with anyone else to build houses or dig wells or plant crops?

Pleasure is a motivator (sometimes called a reinforcer). This means that the pleasure you experience when you do something makes you more likely (motivates you) to do it again. This 'pleasure system' helps you to survive. Animals and humans who have damage to their pleasure system behave very differently from people whose system is working. They are still able to eat, drink, work and reproduce, but they simply do not want to. There is little or no pleasure in these activities, and so they do not bother doing them. They lose motivation to take part in living.

Togetherness
The pleasure people get from loving family relationships motivates them to care for each other and keep the family together.

Cocaine causes a huge rush of pleasure. But, because it has used all the dopamine reserves in your brain (see page 29), it also causes the absence of pleasure. Cocaine users therefore have some experience of a world without pleasure, and it is an unpleasant place. They feel very low and miserable, sad, tired and irritable and these feelings are made worse by the memory of the pleasure they did experience. Pleasure is such a powerful motivator that the cocaine user feels desperate to experience the feeling again. They do not remember that the drug caused the misery as well as the euphoria. So they take more of the drug, desperately trying to recapture the first rush of pleasure. This is the beginning of addiction. Some cocaine users will go on taking cocaine until they overdose or they run out.

'I'm not ready to give up coke yet. I need it too much. Without cocaine the world seems empty to me.'
(Alice, aged 18, cocaine addict)

The development of addiction

Addiction usually develops slowly. People do not get addicted to cocaine the first time they try it. The changes happen gradually, as the brain gets used to the drug and adapts to it. The chemicals in the brain exist in a finely tuned balance and the brain has complicated systems to make sure that the balance is not disturbed. If someone takes a drug like cocaine, which causes large amounts of dopamine to be released, the brain tries to minimize the disruption caused by the drug. It may reduce the amount of dopamine available to be released. Less dopamine available makes the drug user less able to experience pleasure from normal activities, and less able to experience pleasure from taking the drug the next time they try it. They may then take more of the drug, or use it more often, to try to experience the same feelings of pleasure they achieved the first time.

A yearning or longing for a drug is called craving, and various things can trigger a craving for cocaine. Memory is very important. For example, seeing equipment that has been used before to take the drug can be enough to start a craving. This may be injecting equipment, or paper money, which is often rolled into a tube through which to snort cocaine, or any items involved in the user's ritual of cocaine use. Seeing people associated with the drug, or visiting places where the user has taken the drug, or experiencing certain sights, smells, sounds and tastes are all capable of triggering a craving for cocaine.

Eventually the drug takes over the experience of pleasure completely so that, when there is no drug, the brain's 'reward system' does not work properly. Cocaine addicts no longer get pleasure from food, warmth or love – but only from cocaine. The inability to feel pleasure is a powerful reason for keeping on taking a drug. For a few addicts, these changes may be permanent. However, the pleasure system of most cocaine addicts will recover eventually, once they stop taking the drug.

'I've lost my family and friends. All I have now is crack. I have to face up to it, or it will ruin the rest of my life too.'
(Darren, aged 16, crack addict)

Smoking crack
For a crack addict, the drug is more important than their living environment, their family or friends. This addict was photographed on the streets of Panama City, Panama.

What causes addiction?

So why do some people get addicted and not others? Recent research seems to suggest that there may be a part of our genetic makeup that can make us more likely to become addicted. Studies of alcoholics and their children have shown some differences between them and non-alcoholic families. It is thought that some people may inherit a predisposition to become addicted to alcohol and other substances. Animal studies seem to support this idea, but the responsible genes have not yet been fully mapped out. However, having a genetic vulnerability to addiction does not mean that the person will inevitably go on to become an addict. Similarly, not having the gene does not necessarily mean that someone will not become an addict. Environment, behaviour, circumstance and free will all have a part to play.

Self-medication

A large number of cocaine addicts also have psychiatric conditions, such as attention deficit hyperactivity disorder (ADHD), anxiety disorders, mood disorders and personality disorders. One idea is that some people may take cocaine in an attempt to treat themselves for these types of problems. This is called 'self-medication' and may be another cause of addiction.

The term 'addictive personality' is often talked about in magazines, though it is not clear exactly what this personality is. There is some evidence that people who tend to act in particular ways may be more likely than others to develop an addiction. People who are risk-takers and impulsive are more likely to try a drug in the first place, and people who have a tendency to be obsessive (thinking about one particular thing to the exclusion of everything else) find it harder to break addiction.

Environmental factors, such as where you live and who you live or work with, also affect your risk of becoming addicted to drugs. You are more likely to become an addict if you grew up in a household with a substance-abusing parent, if your friends abuse drugs, or if you have been abused as a child. Experimenting with tobacco, cannabis and alcohol at a young age also increase your chances of addiction. Women, in particular, are more likely to abuse drugs when they are older if they suffered abuse as a child. None of this means that you are bound to become an addict if you have experienced problems like these, or if you have a risk-taking or obsessive personality. You always have free choice in what you do with your body and whether or not you take drugs.

Not the type

'I didn't think I'd get addicted to cocaine. I'm not the type. My family weren't badly off and I had a happy childhood. Some guys at college kept going on about how wonderful cocaine was. They said it was OK. They teased me about being scared, so I tried it. It was great – nothing bad happened. I just stayed awake a long time. So I thought this is OK and I started taking it – Saturday night, parties, that sort of thing, just at weekends. Then Monday mornings became harder to handle. Exams were starting, money was running short and I needed some extra help to get through. So I used cocaine to keep me going through the week. It just gradually increased. I felt so bad when I hadn't taken it. All I could think of was getting enough money together to get the next "line". I started dealing a bit, just to friends, and things gradually got out of control. It was like living in a dream. I looked in the mirror one morning and didn't recognize myself. I was not the man I had thought I was going to be. I had no job. I had argued so much with my family that they avoided me and, instead of being someone with prospects, I was a small-time drug dealer with a habit to support. So I made a decision then and there. It had to stop. Get control of my life again or end up in prison or dead. I went to my doctor and got myself into a detox programme. It has not been easy, but I'm not going to let it beat me.'
(Mark, aged 25, recovering cocaine addict)

Peer pressure

Being part of a group who take drugs has a big impact on the likelihood of your becoming addicted. This is partly because some people in the group can probably get hold of drugs for you and partly because of peer pressure. With people who call themselves friends, who use cocaine, it is very hard to resist the pressure to try the drug. Other members of the group may pressure you into joining them. They may say that trying the drug is a test of loyalty to the group, or tease you that you are too scared to try it.

How you react to this pressure can change the course of your life. The pressure to do what your friends want you to do can be enormous. However, you have to decide whether this is the way you want your life to go and whether you are willing to risk your life just to conform with people who care for you so little that they want you to take that risk. Having a clear idea of the risks involved in taking cocaine, and thinking about how you would deal with this sort of situation before it happens, can help you to stay safe and achieve the outcome you want.

Environmental factors can also help people resist addiction. If you have a loving, supportive family and friends, a stable secure life, no family history of substance abuse and a good education, you are far less likely to become an addict. However, it must be remembered that cocaine, and especially crack cocaine, are extremely addictive drugs and whenever cocaine, crack or freebase use has become fashionable, many people from stable loving families with no history of substance abuse have became addicts. Anyone can become addicted to cocaine, no matter who they are or where they live. The next chapter considers how addicts can be helped to give up cocaine.

'I've been offered crack and cocaine but I've never taken them. I'm not that stupid.'
(Sally, aged 17, student)

4 Recovering from addiction
Withdrawal and treatment

Withdrawal

When a drug user stops taking a drug, which they have become used to taking, the process is known as withdrawal. Withdrawal from cocaine use is an unpleasant experience, but it is not usually dangerous or life-threatening, unlike withdrawal from alcohol or heroin. People who have only used cocaine a few times and for limited periods may have very few symptoms of withdrawal.

Cocaine works by over-stimulating the brain and body, and the brain seeks to restore balance by reducing the stimulation. Therefore, when someone stops using cocaine they become exhausted, low and depressed. People who stop taking cocaine often become very hungry too. This is because cocaine tends to decrease the appetite, and so the person may not have eaten properly for quite a while.

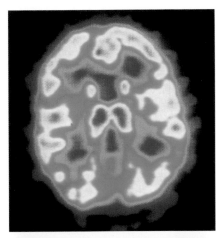

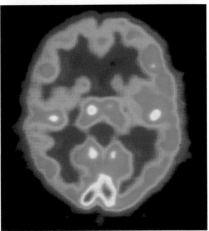

Withdrawal symptoms

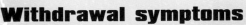

The symptoms of withdrawal from cocaine include:

Agitation
Sadness
Craving for cocaine
Inability to experience pleasure
Hunger
Insomnia with an intense need for sleep
Over-sleeping
Tiredness
Anxiety
Lack of energy

Brain scans
The first of these brain scans shows a slice, front (top) to back, of a normal human brain. The second shows a brain four months after withdrawal from heavy cocaine use. The areas coloured yellow are areas of high activity. The lack of these areas in the ex-cocaine user's brain are the reason for their loss of energy and pleasure.

The biggest problem for people withdrawing from cocaine is the absence of pleasure in their lives. When a heavy user of cocaine stops taking the drug, their brain responds by decreasing the amount of dopamine available and so they are unable to experience pleasure for a while. How long the absence of pleasure lasts depends on several factors, including the length of time over which the user has taken cocaine and how much they took. It also depends on the individual. Some people may be unable to feel pleasure for weeks or months following stopping cocaine.

Taking the first step

Admitting that you are addicted to cocaine is the first step on the road to recovery. Drugs counsellors use a series of questions and answers like the ones listed below to help people who take cocaine, crack and freebase think seriously about how the drug is affecting their lives. Answering yes to any of the questions below is a warning sign that you may have an addiction problem.

- *Do you ever feel you would do anything to get some cocaine/crack/freebase?*
- *Do you ever feel guilty about using cocaine/crack/ freebase?*
- *Do you ever use cocaine/crack/freebase to help you operate or function normally?*
- *Have you ever missed school or work or not fulfilled your responsibilities because you had taken or needed to get cocaine/crack/freebase?*
- *Have you ever stolen anything in order to obtain cocaine/crack/freebase?*
- *Has anyone ever confronted you about using drugs?*

The inability to experience pleasure is a major factor that makes cocaine users go back to using the drug, even though they intended to stop taking it. Life without pleasure, even from food or love, is a very bleak place and the desire to feel pleasure again can be hard to resist. It can cause an intense and sometimes overwhelming craving for the drug. Cravings like this can suddenly occur again many months or even years following withdrawal from heavy cocaine use.

The symptoms that people experience when they stop using cocaine can vary. This is because around 76 per cent of cocaine addicts have at least one psychiatric condition as well as their addiction to cocaine. These conditions include mood disorders, anxiety disorders, personality disorders and attention deficit hyperactivity disorder (ADHD). They can make the feelings associated with withdrawal from cocaine much worse and may result in severe depression and the risk of suicide.

Suicide

The depression suffered by some cocaine addicts leads them to attempt suicide. This is a particular risk for addicts who also use depressant drugs such as alcohol or heroin.

Cocaine addicts are also often addicted to other drugs as well – often alcohol, opiates or amphetamines. This can make withdrawal from cocaine much more dangerous, because of the effects of the other drugs. Alcohol and heroin are both depressant drugs, which can cause the depression following cocaine withdrawal to be unpredictably severe. The person therefore has an increased risk of suicide or self-harm. Because of this, a doctor should supervise people who have a long-established addiction to cocaine during withdrawal from the drug.

Group support
Many people recovering from addiction to drugs find goup counselling a helpful part of their treatment.

Treatment
Drug addiction is treatable and the majority of addicts are able to achieve a complete recovery. Treatment for cocaine addiction needs to be appropriate for each different individual. There are no specific medical treatments to help people withdraw from cocaine, and most doctors do not prescribe any medication for this period. However,

some organizations specializing in narcotic withdrawal have found that it can be very effective for addicts to take vitamin and mineral supplements at the same time as they work through a programme designed to help them learn how to manage in the world without drugs. In general, it seems that the more help an addict is given, the greater the likelihood that they will remain drug-free in the long term.

Because so many people addicted to cocaine have an underlying psychiatric condition, such as attention deficit hyperactivity disorder, withdrawal is much more successful if they have appropriate medication to treat this problem.

'My counsellor made all the difference. Having someone there who really understands how difficult the cravings are has given me the strength to struggle on.' (Amy-Louise, aged 19, recovering crack addict)

The ultimate goal of treatment for cocaine addiction is to help the person to stop using the drug and to return to a normal mental state. Treatment usually involves helping the user move right away from their normal drug-taking environment, and helping them to withdraw safely under medical supervision.

Non-residential support

Non-residential support for recovering cocaine addicts is most suitable for people who already have good support from family and friends and have not been dependent on cocaine for very long. Because of the highly addictive nature of crack cocaine and freebase, addicts to these drugs tend to find it even more difficult to recover from addiction and need lots of support. Recovering addicts can be helped by group counselling, family counselling and behaviour therapy. Behaviour therapy involves learning other ways to behave in situations, different ways to cope with relationships and ways of coping with the difficulties of life without resorting to drugs.

'I became a counsellor for people giving up cocaine after I had gone through the programme myself. I wanted to reach out and help others to beat this terrible illness.' (Alvin, aged 33, addiction counsellor)

Self-help groups, such as Narcotics Anonymous or Cocaine Anonymous, provide a programme that includes group counselling and individual support. These types of programme can be particularly successful, as the support comes from other recovering addicts who can understand the problems involved in overcoming addiction.

Short-term treatment programmes

Short-term treatment programmes usually last between 3 and 6 weeks. Cocaine addicts are supervised during withdrawal, at a residential unit, and afterwards they receive support for the first few months of abstinence from cocaine use. This type of treatment can include exercise programmes and nutritional therapy to help individuals regain their health and strength. It also often includes individual, group and family therapy and education about drugs and addiction and life skills, in order to maximize a recovering addict's chances of staying drug-free.

'I went to a clinic for the first stage of detox. Being right away from the possibility of scoring [buying drugs] meant that I could get through that first stage.' (Ethan, aged 24, recovering cocaine addict)

Therapeutic communities

Therapeutic communities, where people stay for between six and 12 months, can be very successful at helping cocaine addicts overcome addiction. Residential help of this length is more common in the USA than in Europe, which favours shorter programmes. The communities tend to be more suitable for people with a history of long-term heavy cocaine abuse and who have serious difficulty overcoming the psychological problems caused by cocaine, crack and freebase. The treatment focuses on helping individuals to learn how to live in a crime-free, drug-free environment.

Psychological therapy

Psychological therapies include behaviour therapy, where the aim is to change an individual's behaviour, and cognitive therapy, which aims to help people manage the way they think and behave. The ultimate goal of these therapies is to help cocaine addicts to regain control

A new life

Recovering addicts need to remove themselves from the places where they were in contact with the drug. They will need additional support to cope in new surroundings.

over their lives. They often have to relearn how to find pleasure in the natural things of life, such as friends and family, love, food and exercise. Often, cocaine addicts, and particularly those addicted to crack or freebase, need to change their lifestyle completely in order to avoid being back in a situation where they could restart taking the drug. Changing their lifestyle involves making new friends and even moving to a different area. The recovering addicts need support in the development of new relationships. They are also encouraged to join counselling or support groups where they learn strategies to resist temptation and find support to help them stay drug-free.

On-going support

Treating addiction is a long process. Cravings for the drug can last for many months, sometimes for the rest of the person's life. Self-help groups, such as Cocaine Anonymous and Narcotics Anonymous, offer ongoing support for recovering cocaine addicts. This can be vital in helping them resist the temptation to start taking the drug again.

5 Cocaine in today's world
Its impact on society

Although the numbers of people who use cocaine are relatively small, cocaine use has a profound impact on our society. Dealing in cocaine, crack and freebase is associated with crime, violence and prostitution. Crimes are committed by people who produce and smuggle drugs, and by addicts who need to get money to buy the drug. Also, crimes of violence are sometimes committed by people coming down from a crack hit, who are experiencing paranoia.

The trade in cocaine affects the health and welfare of thousands of people around the world, not only those who use the drug. This includes people who are coerced or tricked into smuggling cocaine across borders. Having a family member who is addicted to cocaine can be extremely stressful, and stress can badly affect a person's health, making them more vulnerable to illness. It can also be very stressful living in an area where crack or freebase dealers operate.

Crime scene
Money, a revolver and bags of crack cocaine, seized when police raided a crack house, are signs of the life of crime led by drug dealers.

The law on cocaine

In the USA, cocaine is classified as a Schedule 1 controlled drug. This means that it is illegal to possess or supply the drug to others. It is also illegal to import or export cocaine, crack or freebase, and to allow your premises to be used for the production or supply of the drugs. Penalties vary from state to state.

In the UK, cocaine, crack and freebase are Class A Schedule 2 drugs. It is illegal to buy or possess the drugs without a prescription. It is also illegal to supply the drugs to others, to import, export or process them or to allow your premises to be used for production, supply or taking of the drug. Addiction to cocaine is a notifiable disease in the UK, which means that doctors who have reason to believe that a patient is addicted to cocaine, crack or freebase are obliged to report it to the Home Office.

All members of the European Union classify illegal drugs in accordance with United Nations Conventions. It is therefore illegal to supply, possess, import, export or process cocaine, crack and freebase across the whole of the EU.

Producers, cartels and mules

Most of the cocaine available around the world is grown and processed in one of three countries: Peru, Bolivia and Colombia. However, it is in Colombia that the majority of cocaine is processed. Cocaine production is controlled by a few very rich and powerful gangs, called cartels. Over recent years, cartels from Brazil and Mexico have become more powerful.

Drug cartels are responsible for an enormous amount of misery, not just for the drug addicts they supply with drugs but throughout the whole supply chain. One group of people who are particularly vulnerable are the 'mules'. These are often poor and desperate people, who are

recruited or forced to smuggle cocaine through customs into Europe and America.

Originally, most cocaine was smuggled across the border into the USA from Mexico, or flown in using light aircraft from the Caribbean, particularly Puerto Rico and Haiti. In the late 1980s, the US Drug Enforcement Agency began to warn that the US cocaine market would soon be saturated – in other words, there would be more cocaine available than drug users to buy it. They foresaw that drug cartels would begin to increase the amount of cocaine they smuggled into Europe and Australia. This proved to be the case and in the 1990s the amounts of cocaine seized by UK police and customs officials increased enormously.

Cocaine smugglers use a variety of routes to get the cocaine into a target country. Some cocaine arrives in

The constant search

Customs officers around the world are constantly searching for hidden drug caches. Sniffer dogs are often used, with a high success rate.

Europe through Spain and Portugal, and a large amount arrives in the UK from Jamaica. A report from the United Nations in February 2003 claimed that one in ten of all passengers on flights from Jamaica was smuggling drugs into the UK. Some people feel that this figure underestimates the amount of drug smuggling on these flights. Women caught smuggling drugs into Britain make up more than half of the population in some British women's prisons. Drug cartel bosses are rumoured to pay people £1,500 per trip for trafficking drugs.

Poor women are targeted as mules. A method used to conceal the cocaine they are carrying is for them to swallow packages of up to half a kilogram of the drug, wrapped in the fingers of latex gloves or in condoms. There is a high risk of these packages bursting and, if they do, the carrier receives an enormous dose of cocaine and dies. Nonetheless, many women risk death in this way because they feel that smuggling the drugs is the only way for them to get the money that they desperately need for their families. Consequently, there are a large number of

Coming through customs

'We get loads of smugglers arriving through the airport. Many of the cocaine smugglers come in from Jamaica or other Caribbean countries. Others come in from Spain and Portugal. It's a tragedy. Some of them are so frightened. They look nervous as they come through, especially if they've swallowed packets of cocaine. They are risking their lives. Some of them even come through with their children. They're called mules by drugs gangs. They don't care about the risks these people take. They treat them worse than animals. I feel especially sorry for the women. Some of them are forced to smuggle the drugs. Others are so poor that they think it's worth the risk for the money. Lots of them end up in prison here. Some people are tricked into smuggling drugs. It's slipped into their luggage. Others have drugs sewn into their clothes. It's amazing where they put it.'
(Andrew, customs official)

children in both Jamaica and the UK, whose mother is in jail for smuggling offences. Families are split up and the suffering increases.

Street crime

Since the 1980s, the price of cocaine has gone down and availability has increased, especially of crack and freebase. This has resulted in an increase in cocaine use in some areas of the world, particularly in Europe. In some areas of the UK, in particular, crack cocaine is thought to be growing in popularity and addiction to crack is involved in a wide range of street crimes, including prostitution, mugging, car crime and burglary. However, this effect is very localized. Some inner-city areas suffer from an explosion in crack-related crime, whereas the drug is hardly heard of in other areas.

'These men said, if I did this one trip, I would be rich – able to send my daughter to college. But now I'm stuck here in prison. Ten years ... I won't be able to see my little girl grow up.' (Hester, aged 35, prisoner)

Drugs have a big impact on our society via crime. The British Home Office Department of Research Development and Statistics researched five areas of the UK in 1998 and found that, of all those arrested, 61 per cent had taken at least one illegal drug, 46 per cent tested positive for cannabis, 18 per cent had taken opiates and 10 per cent had taken cocaine. Nearly 50 per cent said that drug use was connected with the crime for which they were arrested. The cost of one drug addict to society, in property crime, theft and prostitution, can be as much as £350,000 per year. The use of alcohol has an even greater effect: 40 per cent of violent crime, 78 per cent of assaults and 88 per cent of criminal damage in Britain is committed under the influence of alcohol.

The spread of crack cocaine use in the UK, the USA and Europe is thought to be related to the activities of Jamaican and other Caribbean gangs. The same groups are thought to be involved in orchestrating the smuggling of cocaine. Fighting between rival gangs in inner-city areas is the cause of much misery and fear and sometimes death.

A crack house

'This used to be a good road – people weren't angels, but you could sleep at night. Now there's crashing and banging all night. I was woken up at 3 am last night by people swearing and screaming. It was frightening. The police came and everything. Mum said that someone had been hurt – a fight, I think. The man over the road has had to move out, but he can't sell his house. It all went wrong after the people over the road moved in. Loads of people are always coming and going. My friend Sam says they are selling drugs – he says it's a crack house. Loads of cars have been broken into and people have had stuff stolen. I'm really scared they'll come in here one day. The people who live next to them are scared to go out and scared to stay in. It's really horrible. The police know about it – they get reported enough. I just don't know what is going to happen.'
(Darcy, aged 14)

Clubbing

There is some evidence that crack cocaine is becoming more popular among clubbers in the UK, especially in Scotland. The British charity DrugScope has said that some clubbers are experimenting with crack cocaine because they are worried about the effects of ecstasy. They mistakenly think that crack is safer. It is not.

The individual cost

Cocaine addiction has a huge effect on the individual addict and their family. Regular use of cocaine, crack and freebase is expensive. Funding an addiction can become the focus of an addict's attention. Everything else is of less importance than the next fix. This can lead to debts building up, stealing from other members of the family, lying and using funds intended for other purposes for drugs and crime.

People who are dependent on cocaine, crack or freebase also often behave in a violent and unpredictable way, which can further isolate them from their families and loved ones. Family and relationships are not as important to the cocaine addict as the next 'hit'. The drug replaces the need for affection and the addict will not let anything get in the way of the next dose.

Family life

'My brother doesn't live with us any more. He got addicted to crack. It all started when he was 16 and he got into what Dad called a "rebellious phase". He became angry, as if he was a different person. He wanted to hurt all of us, even me. I think something must have happened, but he never mentioned anything. He got in with a group of friends – though I wouldn't call them friends. They hung out together and took drugs. Somehow they got my brother to take them too. I didn't think he would do things like that. I thought I knew my brother. I thought he was cleverer than that. They started taking crack. He would come home late, and was angry and frightened. We had to be so careful. Anything I said, he would take the wrong way. It was scary. He started stealing from home to buy drugs. He even stole from me. Mum and Dad had to hide their money and cards. He sold the TV one day – we thought we had been burgled but it turned out that it was him. He sold it to buy more crack. Mum and Dad were so upset. They keep asking what they did wrong, how they can change it. I don't think anything can change it. He ran away from home after that. I feel so angry with him. I hate him, but I wish he would come home.'
(Foley, aged 13)

The distortion of reality caused by the drug prevents addicts from seeing the damage they are doing to the people around them. They often do not recognize that there is anything wrong. Cocaine and crack users have a greater tendency to become aggressive and violent than people who do not take these drugs. This aggression and violence can be especially difficult to live with and are responsible for many relationship breakdowns.

'Crack became like air to me. I couldn't live without it. I had to have it, no matter what. I can't bear to think about some of the things I did to get it. I feel so ashamed.'
(Candy, aged 22, recovering crack addict)

Crack users tend to band together in areas called crack houses. The amount of crime and violence that centres around these areas can destroy communities. In some parts of the world, residents have banded together in order to try to drive crack dealers and users away from their area.

Community spirit
When people band together, they have the power to make their neighbourhood a safe and pleasant place to live.

Keeping the problem in perspective
This chapter has looked at the problems that cocaine use causes in society. However, the level of cocaine use needs to be kept in perspective. The most abused drug in the world is alcohol, which is a legal drug. Despite the lower

price and increased availability of cocaine, crack and freebase today, the vast majority of people will never take these drugs. Cocaine is not a part of normal life, and of the people who do try it, the vast majority will not continue using it or progress to addiction.

Staying in control

Being well-informed is one of the best defences against addiction. If you know the facts about cocaine and crack, and their potential for harm and addiction, you are less likely to be fooled by someone trying to tell you that the drugs are harmless. It is a good idea to think about situations you might find yourself in, before they happen. If you were at a party and someone offered you a crack-laced cigarette, or a line of cocaine, what would you do? If you want to try it, are you fully aware of the risks you are taking? Do you know what it is you are being offered?

Cocaine and crack risks: the facts

- You can never be sure exactly what you are taking.
- Drugs are often mixed with other substances, such as talcum powder, to dilute the drug and increase the profit for the dealer.
- Both crack and cocaine have the potential to kill you with just one dose.
- You do not know how pure a substance is, so it is easy to overdose.
- You cannot be sure what effect the drug will have on you, even if you have taken it before.
- Mixing drugs is very dangerous, especially taking drugs at the same time as alcohol or cold medicines.
- Sharing needles and syringes carries serious risk of infection from diseases such as HIV and hepatitis.
- There is a real risk of being caught by the police. You may be arrested and prosecuted.
- If you are found in possession of cocaine, crack or other drugs, you risk losing your job or being excluded from school.
- There is a risk to other members of your family. Your parents may be arrested and charged if drugs are found in their home.
- You run the risk of becoming addicted.

If you do not want to take it, how will you say 'no'? Practising what to do in different situations is called role-play. Role-playing with friends is helpful, as you can discuss different ways of handling a situation. It is impossible to say exactly what to do in each situation, because your life, experience and environment are different to anyone else's.

If someone approaches you to sell cocaine or other drugs, or you are worried that a friend has taken drugs, then you need to tell someone. It is usually best to tell your parents, but if you feel unable to talk to them, then a teacher or youth worker may be able to help. In some places there are groups of drugs counsellors your own age, to whom you can go for advice or support. Do not worry in silence. There are some useful points of contact in the resources section on page 62.

Role play

Role-playing different situations where you may be offered drugs prepares you to deal confidently with real-life events.

Glossary

addiction — when someone uses a drug repetitively and compulsively, even though it has negative effects.

addictive — having the potential to cause addiction.

alcohol — an intoxicating liquid formed when sugar is fermented by yeast.

anaesthetics — drugs that reduce the ability of the body to experience pain.

atherosclerosis — porridge-like fat that coats the inside of blood vessels and makes them narrower.

caffeine — a stimulant drug present in tea, coffee and chocolate.

circulatory system — the system involved in moving blood around the body. It includes the heart, veins, arteries and capillaries.

coma — unconsciousness.

compulsively — following a strong, irrational urge to act in a particular way.

convulsions — involuntary violent spasms of the muscles of the body.

craving — a desperate and urgent longing.

dependent — a person is said to be dependent on a drug when they have a compelling desire, physical or psychological, to keep taking it.

depressant drugs — drugs that depress the nervous system rather than exciting it.

depression — a treatable medical condition where the individual feels hopeless, inadequate and unhappy. It is usually accompanied by sleep problems and appetite changes.

derivative — something that is produced from something else.

detox — detoxification, the act of ridding the body of toxins or poisons.

dopamine — a neurotransmitter that is involved in purposeful movement, hormone release, euphoria and the way we experience pleasure.

drug — a chemical that is taken into a person's body in order to change their physical or mental state.

euphoria — a feeling of extreme wellbeing and elation.

genetic — carried or passed on through the genes. Genes are parts of your body cells containing characteristics that are inherited from your biological parents and ancestors.

hallucination — the perception of something that is not really there. This can involve seeing, hearing, smelling, tasting or feeling.

heart attack — when the heart suddenly stops working properly. Heart attacks are a medical emergency and can result in death.

hepatitis — a highly infectious virus passed on by contact with body fluids such as blood or sperm. It causes serious inflammation of the liver and can be fatal.

high — slang for the experience of being under the influence of a psychoactive drug.

hit — slang for the first 'rush' or experience after taking a drug.

HIV — Human Immunodeficiency Virus, a virus that attacks part of the body's immune system. It is passed on by contact with infected blood, sperm or saliva.

hormones — a group of chemicals produced by the body, which affect the way the body functions.

infertility — biological inability to have children.

miscarriage — premature ending of a pregnancy, when the foetus dies.

mucous membranes — body tissue that produces mucus in order to lubricate an area and protect it from infection. The lungs are one organ of the body that has a mucous membrane.

narcotics — drugs that affect the central nervous system, producing dizziness, euphoria and ultimately unconsciousness and death.

neuro-transmitters — chemicals that transmit a message across a junction (synapse) between two nerves. They are mainly found in the brain and spinal cord.

noradrenalin — a neurotransmitter that regulates the body's physical and mental reaction to stress.

opiates — drugs produced from the sap of the opium poppy, such as codeine, morphine and heroin.

overdose — taking too much of a drug. This usually causes physical or mental damage.

paranoia — a mental condition where you think that everyone is out to get you. Intense irrational fear and suspicion.

Parkinson's disease — a disease that causes a lack of dopamine. This results in tremor, mask-like expression, loss of coordination, fatigue and depression.

psychedelic movement — 1960s movement where people became interested in the mind-altering properties of drugs and wanted to explore the creative potential of their drug-induced experiences in art, music and philosophy.

psychiatrist — a person medically qualified to treat diseases of the mind.

psychoactive — affecting the brain and behaviour.

psychosis — a serious mental condition usually involving illusions, confusion, delusions and hallucinations, with the sufferer not realizing that they are ill.

ritual — a ceremony or sequence of actions performed the same way every time, to make the event seem special.

serotonin — a neurotransmitter that regulates the body clock, appetite, sleep patterns and body temperature.

smoking — breathing in the chemicals produced by burning drugs.

snorting — sniffing a substance into the nose.

stereotypical movements — repetitive persistent movements that the individual is unable to control.

stillbirth — a baby that is born dead.

stimulants — drugs that 'stimulate' (increase the activity level of) the body and mind.

stroke — a sudden event that causes the rupture of blood vessels in the brain.

Resources

Further reading

C. Kuhn, S. Swartzwelder and W. Wilson, *Buzzed, The straight facts about the most used and abused drugs from alcohol to ecstasy*, W. W. Norton & Company, New York, London, 1998.

Aidan Macfarlane and Ann McPherson, John Alstrop, *The new diary of a teenage health freak*, Oxford Paperbacks, 1996.
Funny, easy-to-read introduction to all health education issues including drugs.

Sarah Lennard-Brown, *Health Issues: Drugs*, Hodder Wayland, 2001.
The facts and issues surrounding illegal drug use.

www.mindbodysoul.gov.uk
British government website, for 14-16 year-olds giving information about drugs and wellbeing.

Organizations

DrugsScope
Waterbridge House, 32-36 Loman Street,
London SE1 0EE
Telephone: 020 7928 1211
www.drugscope.org.uk
An independent British charity which researches drug-related issues and advises on policy-making and drugs prevention and information issues.
It has an excellent data base of information about all drugs.

Cocaine Anonymous World Service
PO Box 2000, Los Angeles, CA 90049-8000 USA
www.ca.org

Narcotics Anonymous
202 City Road, London EC1V 2PH
Telephone: 020 7251 4007
UK helpline: 010 7730 0009

Sources

The following sources were used in researching this book:

M. Bloor and F. Wood (editors), *Addictions and problem drug use*, Jessica Kingsley Publishers, London, 1998.
D. Emmett and G. Nice, *Understanding Drugs,* Jessica Kingsley Publishers, London, 1998.
S. G. Forman, *Coping skills and interventions for children and adolescents*, Jossey-Bass Publishers, San Francisco, 1993.
C. Kuhn, S. Swartzwelder and W. Wilson, *Buzzed, The straight facts about the most used and abused drugs from alcohol to ecstasy*, W. W. Norton & Company, New York, London, 1998.
A. Macfarlane and A. McPherson, *Teenagers, the Agony, the Ecstasy, the Answers*, Little Brown and Company, London, 1999.

World Health Organization:
www.who.int/whr/1999/en/pdf/chapter5.pdf

British Home Office:
www.homeoffice.gov.uk

Index